DAD

I WROTE THIS BOOK ABOUT

YOU

THIS BOOK WAS WRITTEN BY

_____

_____

_____

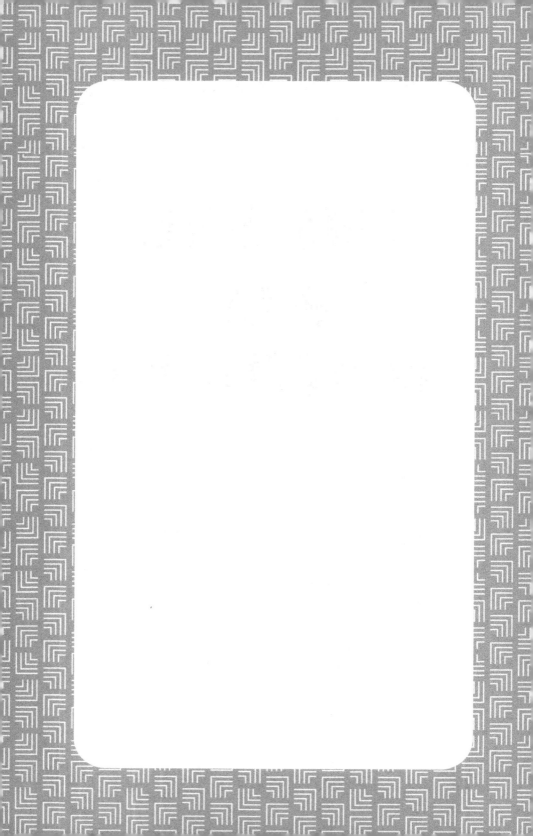

I LOVE IT
WHEN YOU

_____

_____

_____

_____

OUR FAVORITE THING TO DO IS

_____

_____

_____

_____

YOU SMILE WHENEVER I

_____

_____

_____

_____

IT WAS SO MUCH FUN WHEN WE

_____

_____

_____

_____

YOU ALWAYS HELP ME

_____

_____

_____

_____

I LOVE IT WHEN YOU TELL ME

_____

_____

_____

_____

YOU ARE REALLY HAPPY WHEN

_____

_____

_____

_____

I LOVE IT WHEN WE

_____

_____

_____

_____

THE FUNNIEST THING THAT YOU DO IS

_____

_____

_____

_____

YOU WILL ALWAYS BE THE BEST

_____

_____

_____

_____

I LOVE IT WHEN YOU CALL ME

_____

_____

_____

_____

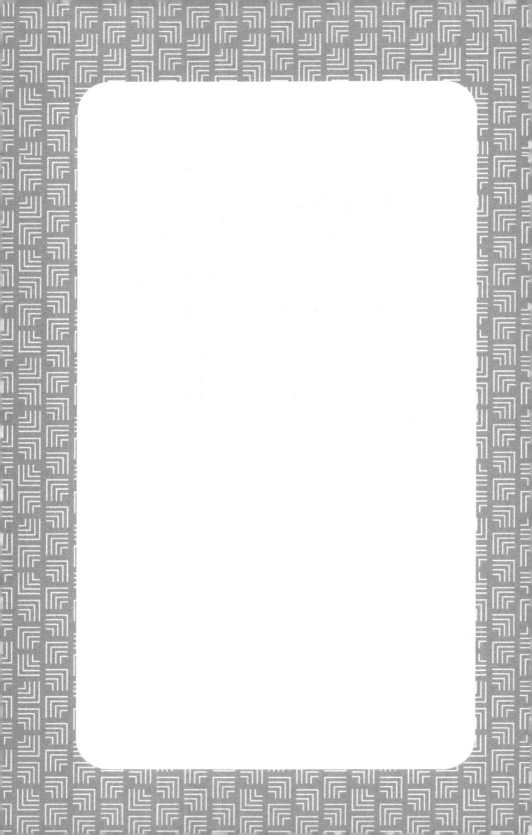

YOU HAVE TAUGHT ME HOW TO

_____

_____

_____

_____

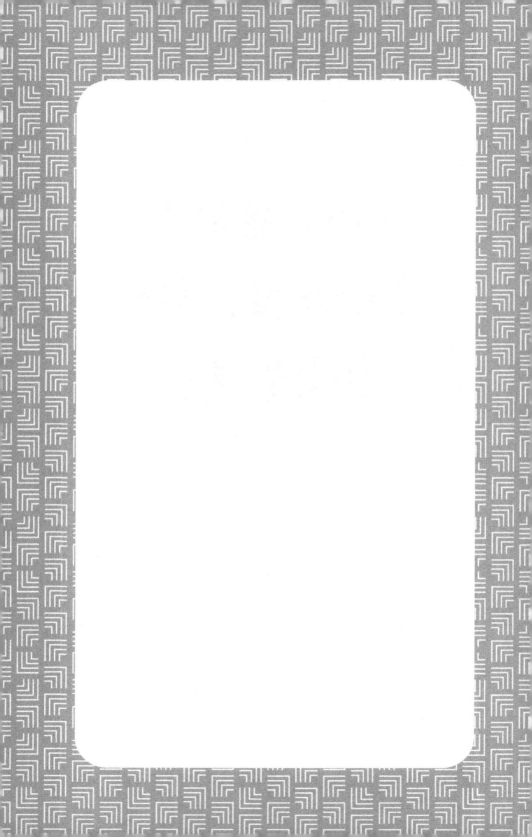

I AM PROUD THAT YOU ARE

_____

_____

_____

_____

YOUR FAVORITE FOOD IS

_____

_____

_____

_____

IT IS SO GOOD THAT YOU ALWAYS

_____

_____

_____

_____

OUR FAVORITE GAME TO PLAY IS

_____

_____

_____

_____

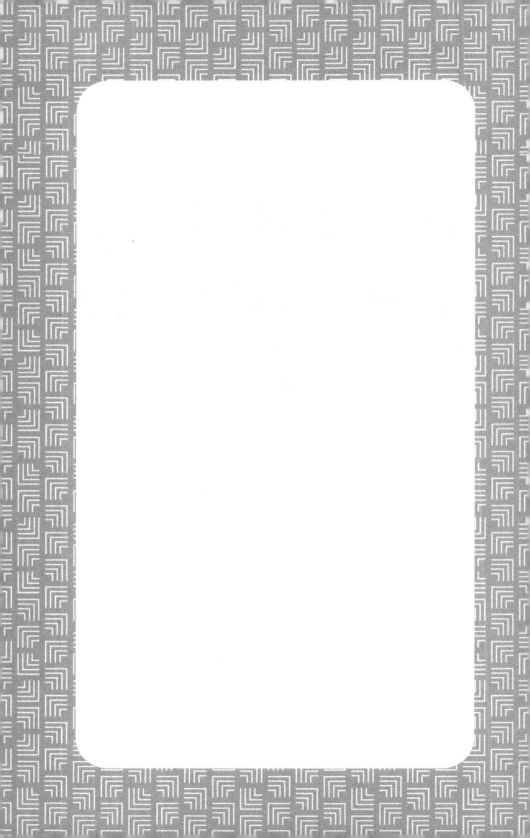

I LOVED IT WHEN WE WENT TO

_____

_____

_____

_____

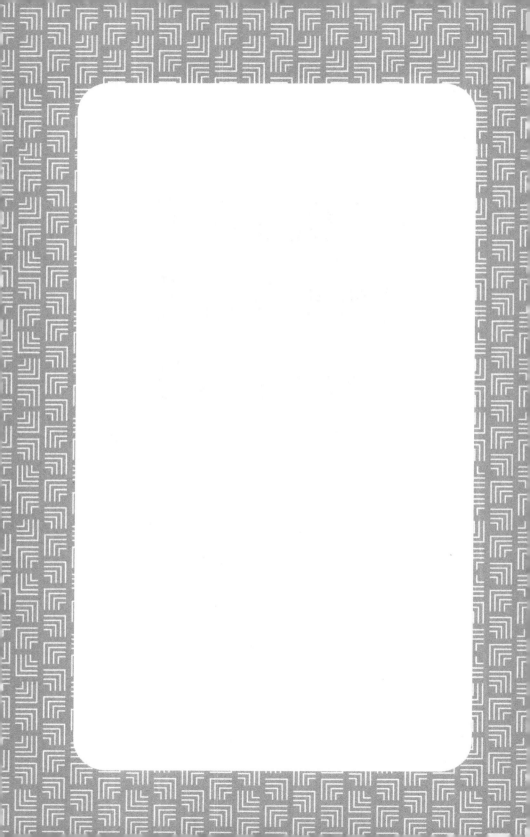

THANK YOU
SO MUCH FOR

_____

_____

_____

_____

ONE DAY I WOULD LOVE TO BUY YOU

_____

_____

_____

_____

SOMETIMES YOU MAKE FUNNY

_____

_____

_____

_____

I WISH WE HAD MORE TIME TO

_____

_____

_____

_____

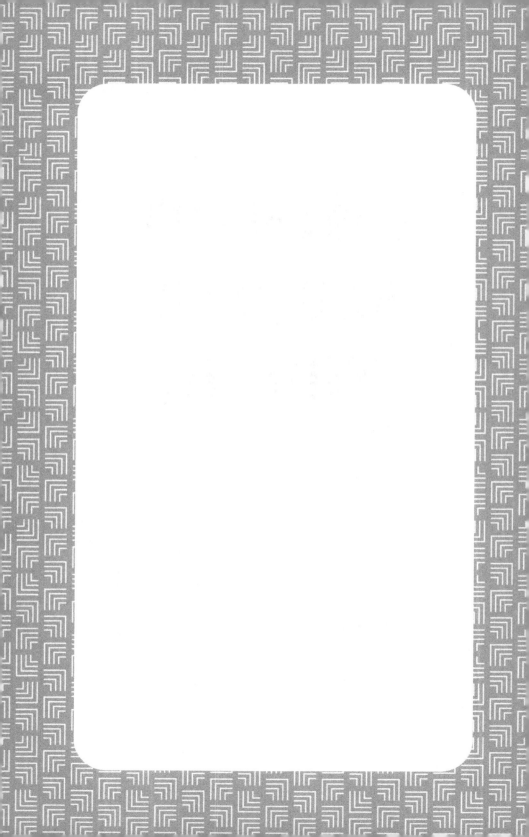

I THINK YOU ARE SO COOL BECAUSE

_____

_____

_____

_____

YOU ARE THE KIND OF PERSON WHO

_____

_____

_____

_____

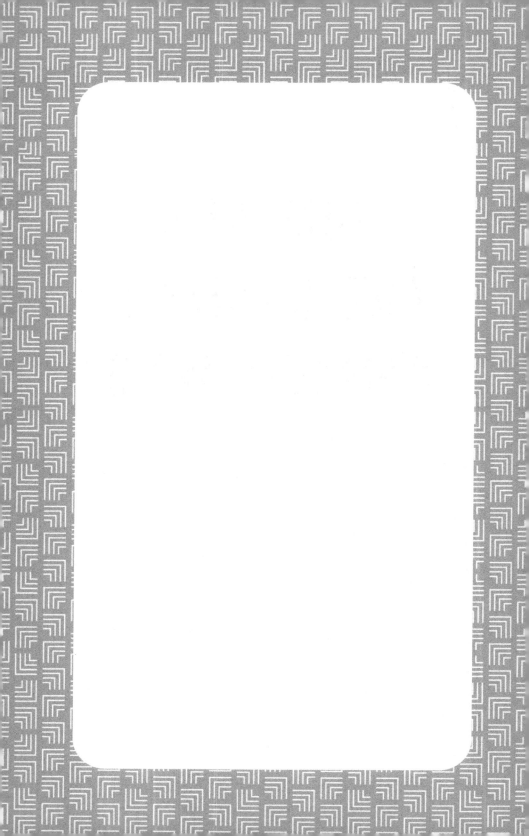

THE BEST THING ABOUT YOU IS

_____

_____

_____

_____

YOU ALWAYS SMILE EVEN WHEN

_____

_____

_____

_____

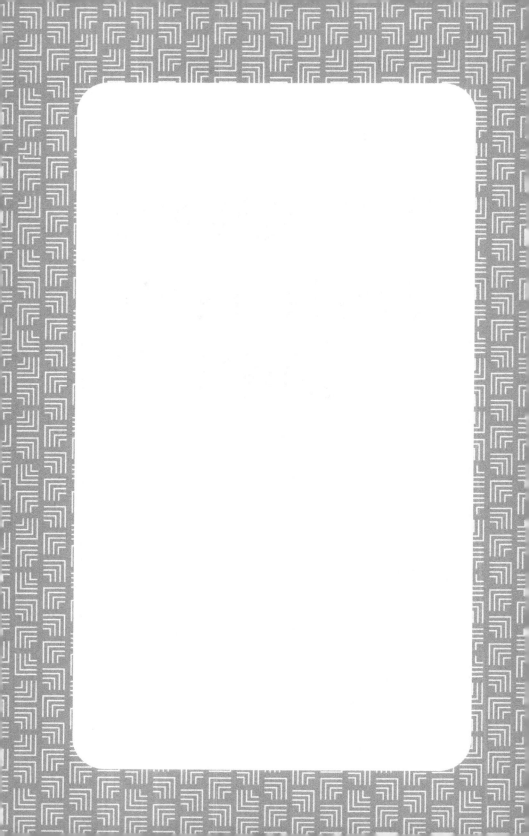

YOU ARE REALLY GOOD AT

_____

_____

_____

_____

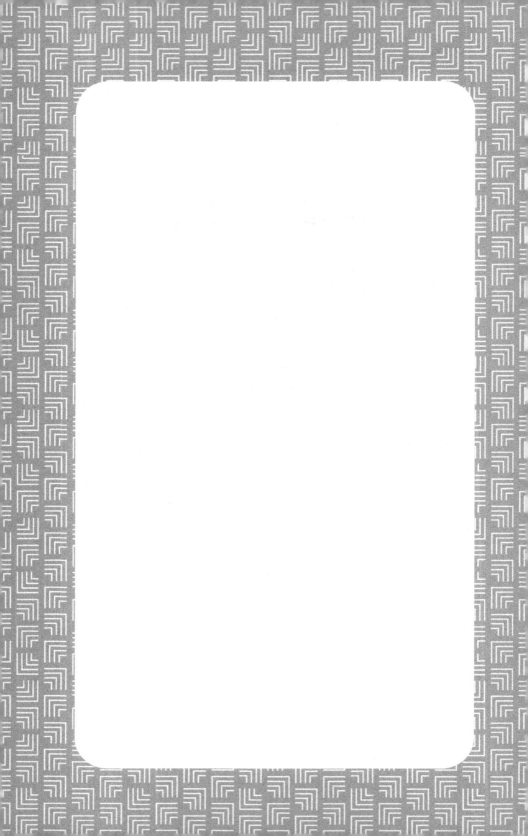

I KNOW YOU LOVE ME BECAUSE YOU

_____

_____

_____

_____

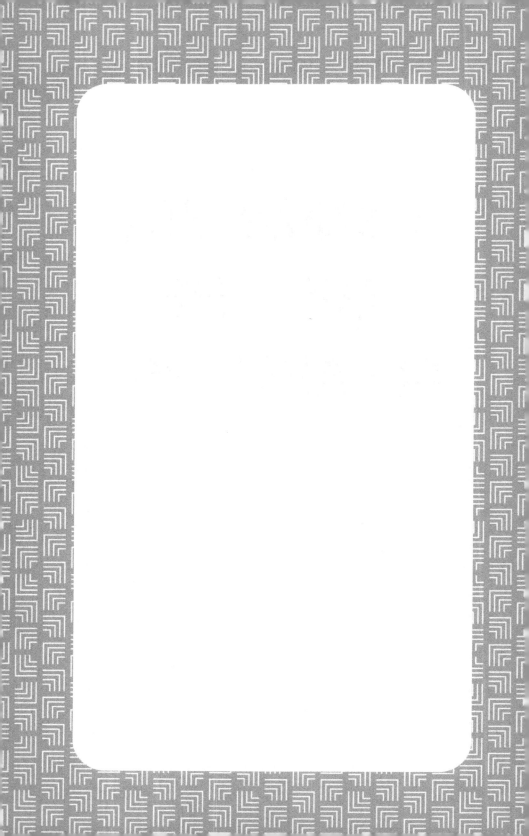

YOU ARE
SO SMART
BECAUSE YOU

_____

_____

_____

_____

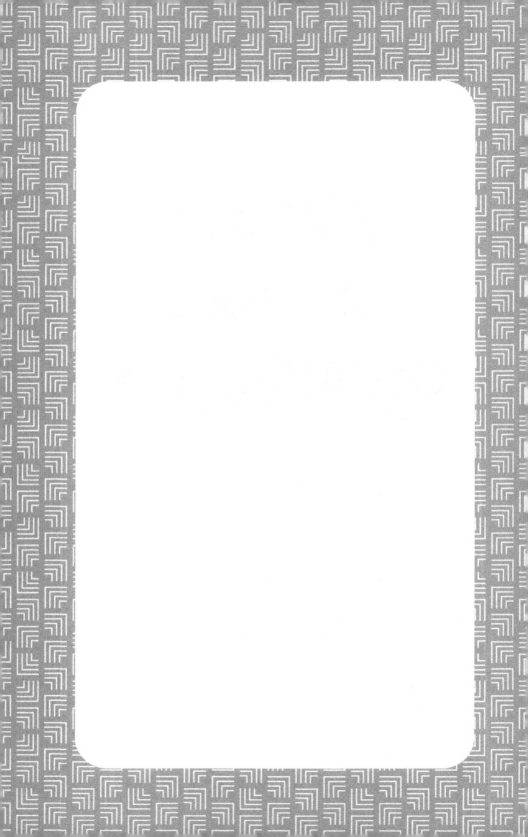

I LOVE
HOW YOU
ALWAYS

_____

_____

_____

_____

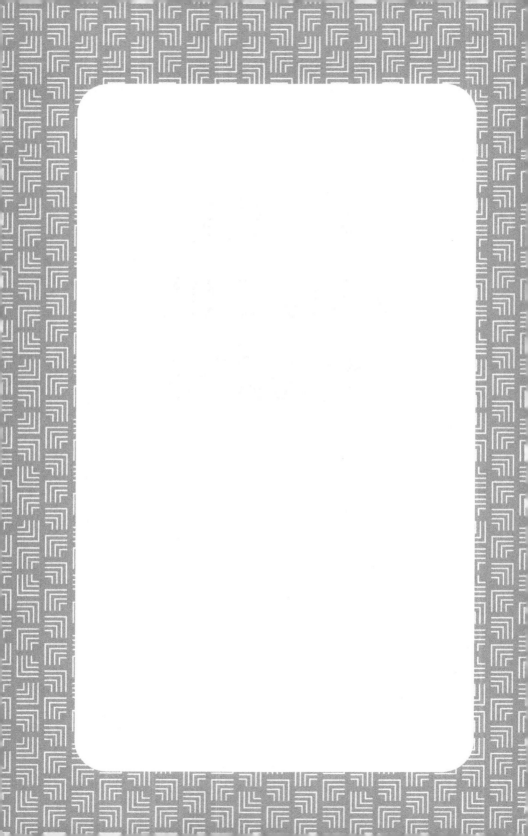

YOU
LOVE IT
WHEN I

_____

_____

_____

_____

IT WAS SO COOL WHEN YOU GAVE ME

_____

_____

_____

_____

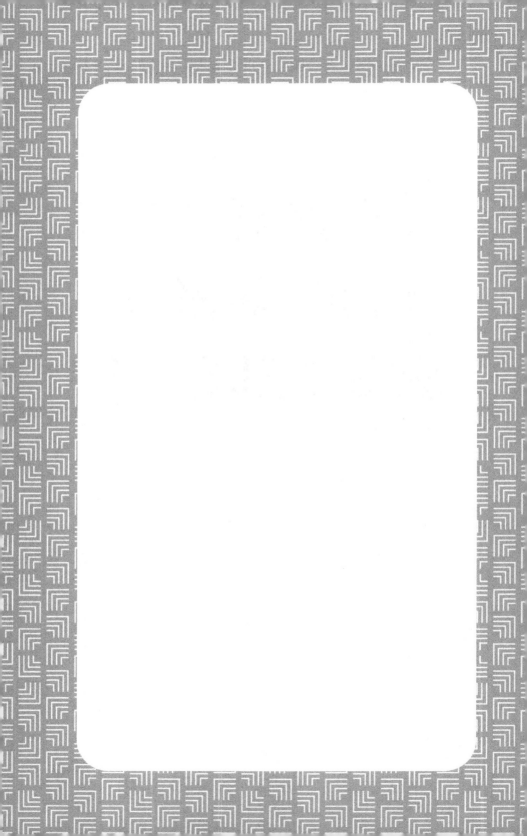

I CAN'T WAIT UNTIL WE

_____

_____

_____

_____

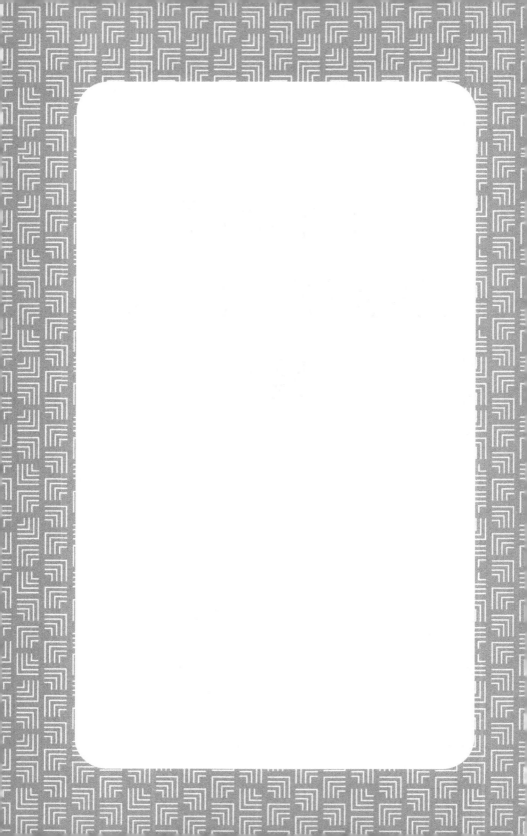

WHEN I THINK OF YOU I ALWAYS

_____

_____

_____

_____

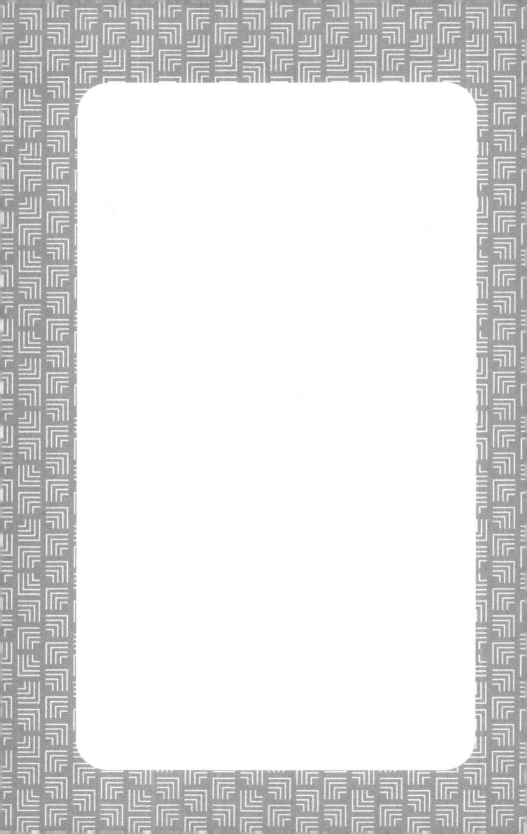

DAD
I LOVE YOU
MORE THAN

_____

_____

_____

_____

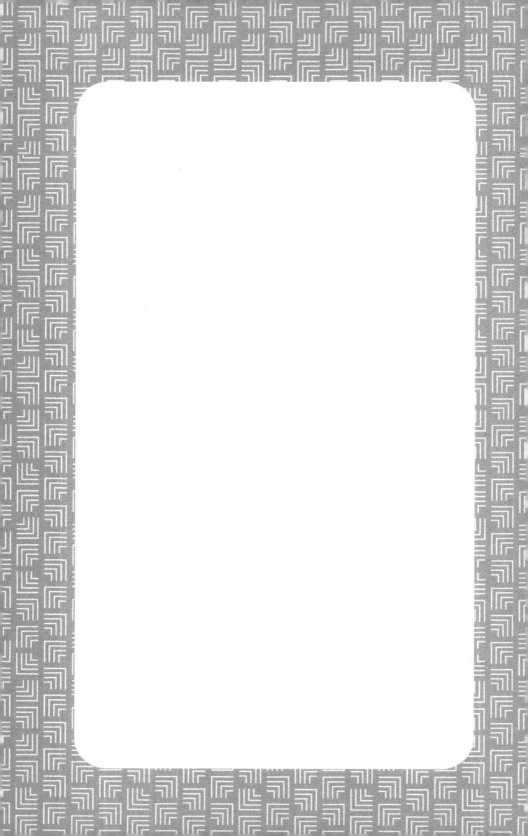

MY FRIENDS THINK THAT YOU ARE

_____

_____

_____

_____

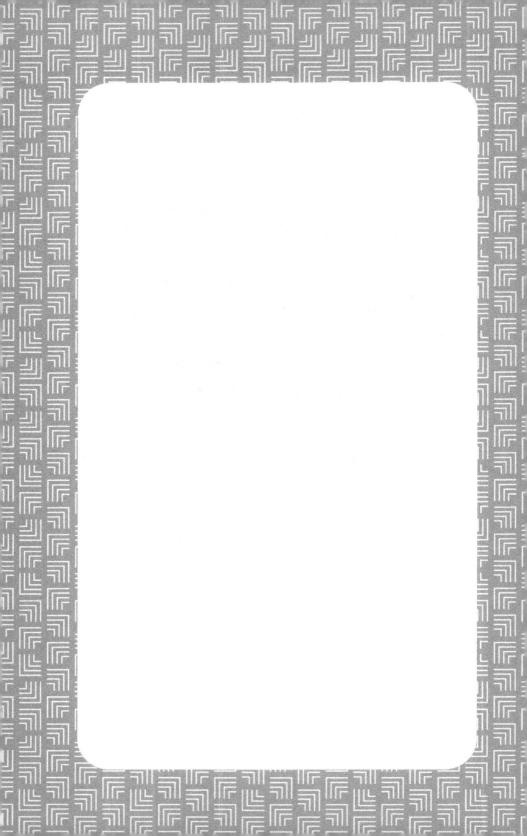

YOU ARE SUCH A GOOD

_____

_____

_____

_____

I LOVED IT WHEN YOU MADE

_____

_____

_____

_____

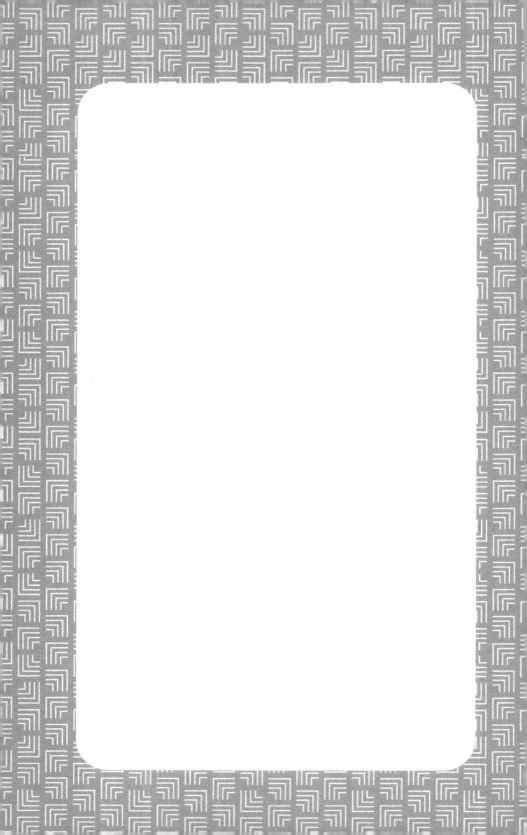

YOU INSPIRE ME TO

_____

_____

_____

_____

YOUR FAVORITE TV SHOW IS

_____

_____

_____

_____

YOU LOVE ME BECAUSE

_____

_____

_____

_____

YOU ALWAYS MAKE ME LAUGH WHEN

_____

_____

_____

_____

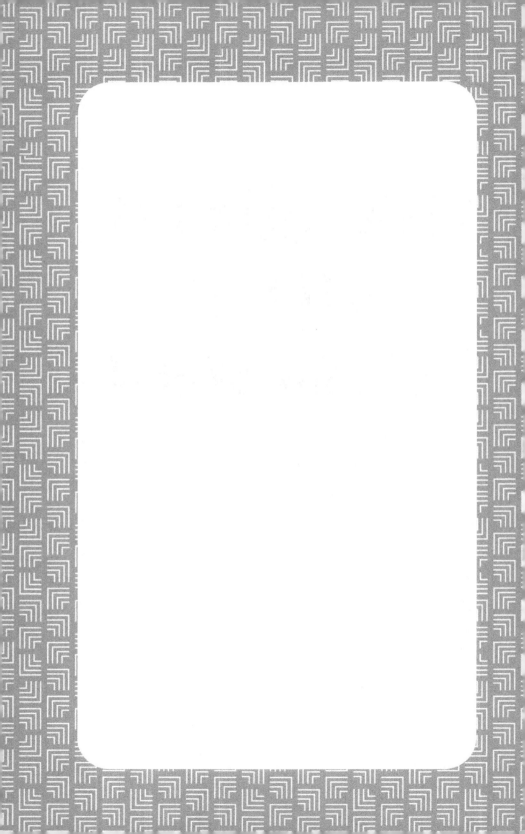

WHEN PEOPLE MEET YOU THEY THINK

_____

_____

_____

_____

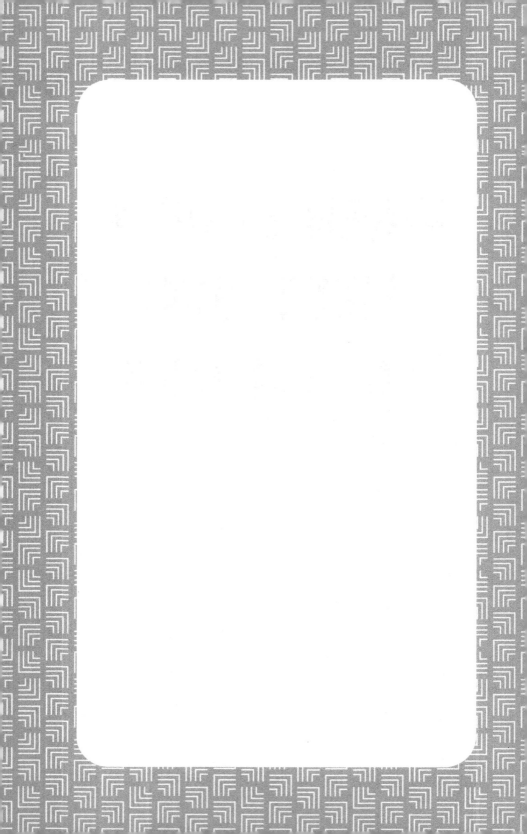

YOU SHOULD WIN FIRST PRIZE FOR

_____

_____

_____

_____

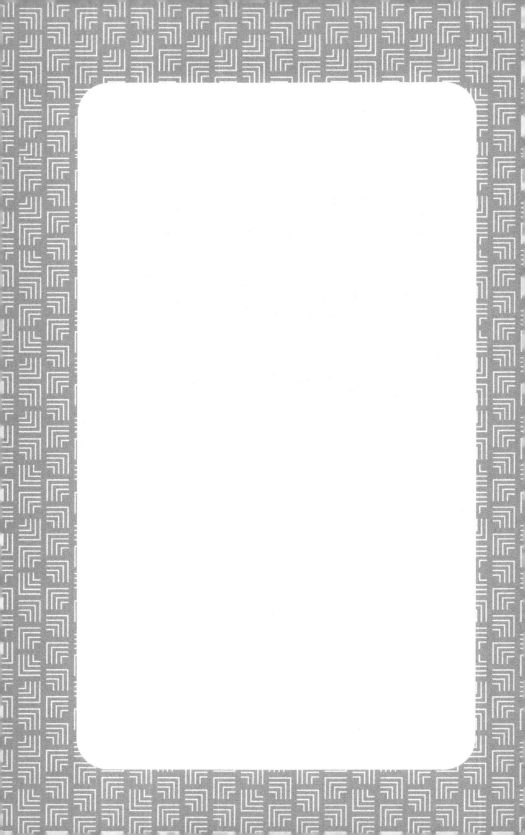

YOU WERE PROUD OF ME WHEN I

_____

_____

_____

_____

I LOVE HEARING YOUR STORIES FROM

_____

_____

_____

_____

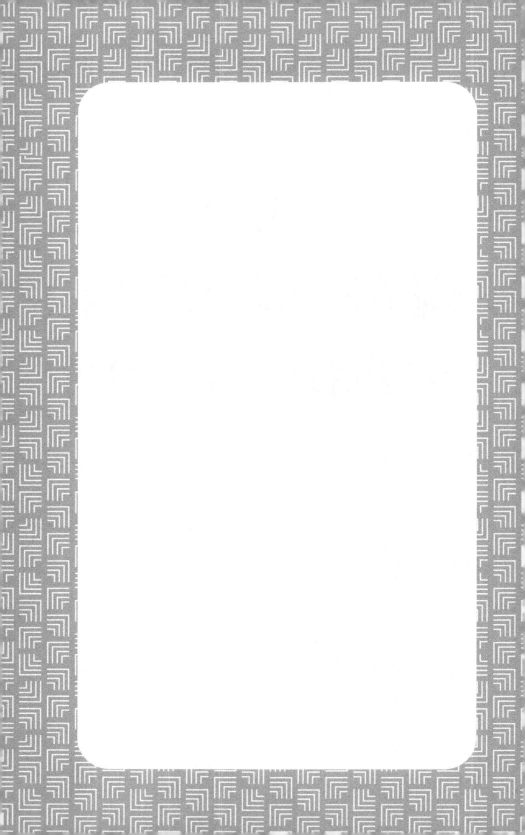

YOU ARE SO SPECIAL TO ME BECAUSE

_____

_____

_____

_____

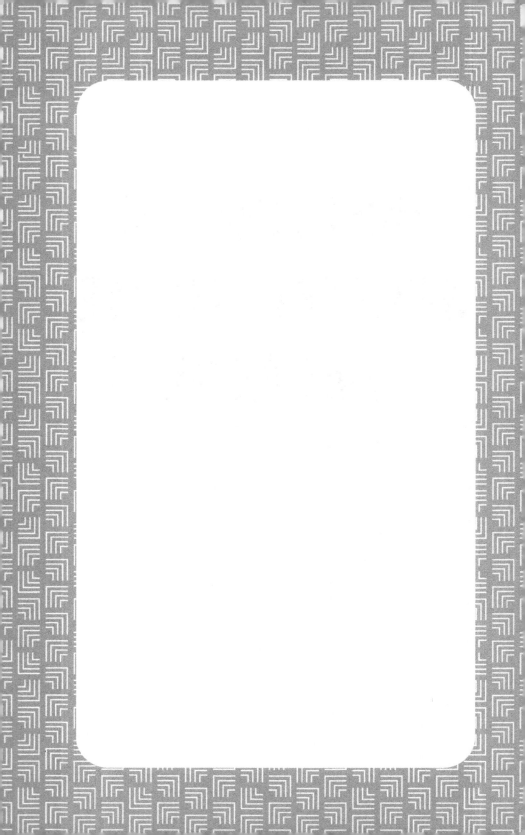

I LOVE IT WHEN YOU COOK

_____

_____

_____

_____

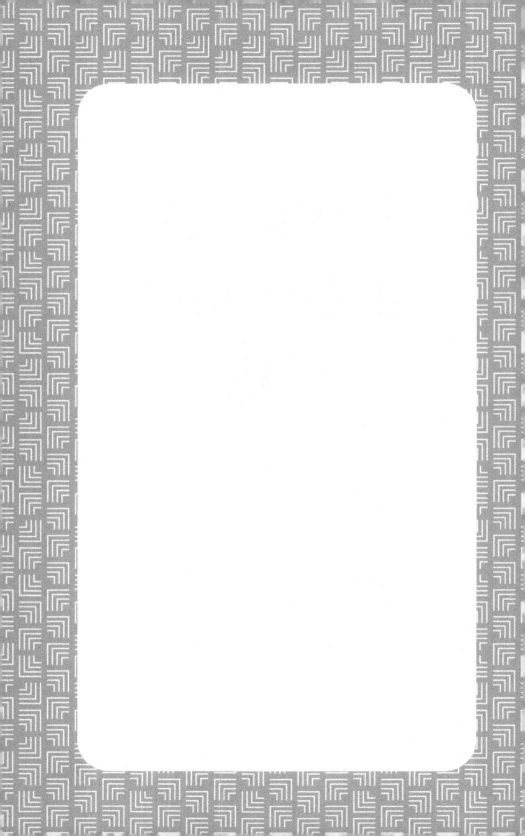

THANK YOU
FOR BEING
THE BEST

_____

_____

_____

_____

YOU MAKE ME FEEL SPECIAL WHEN

_____

_____

_____

_____

YOUR FAVORITE SAYING IS

_____

_____

_____

_____

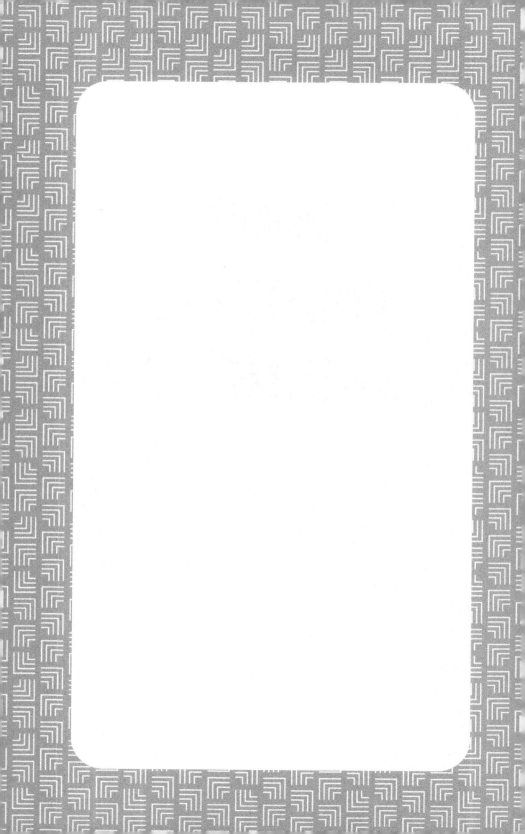

IT'S GREAT FUN WHEN WE

_____

_____

_____

_____

MOST OF ALL, DAD, I LOVE YOU BECAUSE

_____

_____

_____

_____

Made in United States
North Haven, CT
17 December 2022

29088172R00063